122

LIFE WORKS!

FUSION

COUNT ON ME

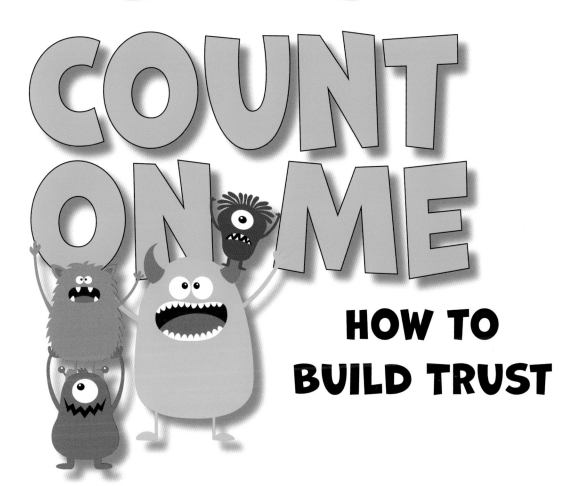

HOW TO BUILD TRUST

by Sloane Hughes

BEARPORT
PUBLISHING

Minneapolis, Minnesota

Credits: Cover background, © cammep/Shutterstock; cover (monsters)1, 4, 8–9, 11, 13, 15–16, 19, 21–23, © world of vector/Shutterstock; 2–3, 12–19, 24 (background), © fishStok/Shutterstock; 4 (eggs), © svtdesign/Shutterstock; 5, © Veronica Louro/Shutterstock; 6, © fizkes /Shutterstock; 7T, © Akkalak Aiempradit/Shutterstock; 7B, © Silvia Moraleja/Shutterstock; 8, © Brocreative/Shutterstock; 9 (ice cream), © Shany Muchnik/Shutterstock; 13, © JR-50/Shutterstock; 15 (jellyfish), © kiwi9314 /Shutterstock; (bread), © vivat/Shutterstock; 16, © SeventyFour/Shutterstock; 17, © fizkes/Shutterstock; 19, © Nataliia Zhekova/Shutterstock; 22–23, © Rawpixel.com/Shutterstock.

Library of Congress Cataloging-in-Publication Data

Names: Hughes, Sloane, author.
Title: Count on me : how to build trust / Sloane Hughes.
Description: Fusion Books. | Minneapolis, Minnesota : Bearport Publishing Company, 2022. | Series: Life works! | Includes index.
Identifiers: LCCN 2021039146 (print) | LCCN 2021039147 (ebook) | ISBN 9781636914251 (library binding) | ISBN 9781636914305 (paperback) | ISBN 9781636914350 (ebook)
Subjects: LCSH: Trust--Juvenile literature. | Friendship--Juvenile literature.
Classification: LCC BF575.T7 H84 2022 (print) | LCC BF575.T7 (ebook) | DDC 158.2--dc23
LC record available at https://lccn.loc.gov/2021039146
LC ebook record available at https://lccn.loc.gov/2021039147

For more information, write to Bearport Publishing, 5357 Penn Avenue South, Minneapolis, MN 55419. Printed in the United States of America.

CONTENTS

HELPING OUT!

Being a good friend means being there for others. We help others with what they need.

I need three eggs.

1, 2, 3! You can count on me!

We say "You can count on me to be a friend!" with our words and actions.

TRUST IN ME

When we help others, they can start to **trust** us. This means our friends and family know we will be there for them. They learn they can trust us when we . . .

Tell the truth

Do what we
say we will do

Keep secrets
for our friends

Think of someone you trust. How do you know you can trust them?

7

I HEAR YOU

Others also know they can count on us when we are good listeners. This makes them know we care.

Good listeners hear what friends say. They listen closely to make sure they understand.

LISTEN AND LEARN

Listening helps us know what others think and feel. Practice with a friend.

TRY IT:

CAN YOU COPY?

2. Without looking, ask them what they drew.

3. Listen carefully and ask questions. Try to make the same picture.

1. Ask a buddy to draw a simple picture.

4. Show each other your pictures. How close did you get?

ACTION HERO!

Listening well helps us know what others want and need. Then, what can we do for our friends? It's time to act!

When we say we will do something, it's important to do it. This shows others they can trust us. Become an action hero!

Trust is built. Each time we do something like we said, we make it stronger.

Are you a super friend?

EVERYBODY HAS A PART

Trust your friends to help make a tasty lunch.

TRY IT

LUNCH TIME

2. Decide what you want to eat. What **ingredients** will you need?

3. Split up the ingredients so everyone is in charge of bringing something.

1. Plan a picnic lunch with friends.

4. Come together and make your meal!

RESPECT

Showing respect lets others know they are important. We like them for who they are.

When we respect people, we care about their feelings.

Everyone should get our respect. It helps them know they can trust us.

We show respect by being kind and **polite**.

KEEP RESPECT HANDY

There are a lot of ways to show respect. Come up with a handful.

TRY IT

RESPECT REMINDER

1. Use a pencil to trace your hand on a sheet of paper.

2. Think of five ways to show respect.

3. Write one way in each traced finger.

Listen while a friend speaks.

Open the door for others!

19

SOMEONE ELSE'S SHOES

Want a simple rule for respect? Always treat others the way we want to be treated. We can use **empathy** to do this. In our minds, we put ourselves in someone else's shoes!

With empathy, we **imagine** what it feels like to be our friend. Then, we can understand and help them.

How does empathy work?

We think about when we went through something similar.

We remember how it made us feel.

Then, we imagine how someone else feels.

Ask someone how they're feeling. Have you ever felt the same way?

THE POWER OF WE

Usually, trust goes both ways. When we show others they can trust us, they often show us we can trust them, too.

Respect is cool.

Counting on those around us means
we can get help when we need it. It
makes every day a little easier. Let's
count on *we*!

GLOSSARY

empathy the understanding and sharing of the feelings and experiences of another

imagine to picture something in your mind

ingredients the different things that are used to make food

polite showing good manners

repeating saying something after someone else has said it

trust to believe that somebody or something is good or true

INDEX